BASKETBALL

BASKETBALL

MUCH MORE
THAN JUST A

GAME

LARRY McKENZIE

authorHOUSE®

AuthorHouse™
1663 Liberty Drive
Bloomington, IN 47403
www.authorhouse.com
Phone: 1-800-839-8640

First published by AuthorHouse 10/5/2011

ISBN: 978-1-4634-3753-4 (sc)
ISBN: 978-1-4634-3752-7 (hc)

Library of Congress Control Number: 2011915909

Printed in the United States of America

Cover Design: Chris Liskiewicz - Designcrl

Dedication

This book is dedicated to the memories of:

- My grandfather, William Arnold Moray Jones, who modeled unconditional love and taught me the true meaning of being a man.

- My pops, Lawrence McKenzie, a first-generation American citizen who lived the American dream and was a true inspiration to his kids and grandkids.

- James Pope Jr., my father-in-law, who was truly an amazing man. He dedicated the majority his life as a freedom fighter, serving twenty-five-plus years in the US Army, all while raising nine kids and taking care of a wife challenged by multiple sclerosis.

- My mentor and second father, John K. Cameron, who taught me the importance of preparation; I can still hear him reminding me, "Plan your work, and work your plan."

- Myra Smith-Flake, who we lost to breast cancer, a true angel who introduced me to my wife, Dianne, and helped start a new journey in my life .We are so fortunate to have shared in her life, if only for a season.

Lawrence McKenzie 1950 Booker T Washington Basketball Team
Pop McKenzie (Far Right)

"If you're trying to achieve, there will be roadblocks. I've had them; everybody has them. But obstacles don't have to stop you.

If you run into a wall, don't turn around and give up. Figure out how to climb it, go through it, or work around it.

I've always believed that if you put in the work, the results will come. I don't do things half-heartedly, because I know if I do, then I can expect half-hearted results.

I play to win, whether during practice or a real game, and I will not let anything get in the way of me and my competitive enthusiasm to win."

—Michael Jordan

Table of Contents

Foreword

By
Tubby Smith

Coach McKenzie and I have a lot in common when it comes to the game of basketball. Both of us have played the game, coached the game, and coached our sons. We also have in common the fact that we both coached *his* son. I had the good fortune of coaching Lawrence (one of the most coachable players I've ever worked with) my first year at the University of Minnesota. However, our most unmistakable similarity is that what originally started out as a personal love for the game quickly became a desire to spread and implement that love throughout generations to come. That is how I know this book and the experiences shared in it are very personal for Coach McKenzie and are very valuable to you.

You can feel Coach McKenzie's passion for the game as you flip through the pages of *Basketball: Much More than Just a Game*. This is an opportunity to get an authentic look at the game through the eyes of a coach who has been to the top—winning four Minnesota state high school basketball championships at Minneapolis Patrick Henry High School. This book gives us all a "behind the scenes" look at the grind and determination it takes to be an elite athlete regardless of the level.

His ability to effortlessly communicate the essentials of the game is as evident in his writing as it is on the sidelines. Coach McKenzie shares his insight into what it takes in this day and time to be a successful coach, athlete, parent, and person.

Today, the game of basketball is being impacted by many different entities: family, high school coaches, AAU coaches, college coaches, workout gurus, and agents. This book should be used as a tool for players and parents navigating the game and the professionals associated with it.

Coach McKenzie gives an in-depth look at the business surrounding basketball and offers ideas for how the next generation can leave a legacy through the game and in life. He addresses several topics—from having fun to incorporating the basic fundamentals—and there is something for each and every one of us to learn.

Shedding a light on both the good and the bad aspects of basketball, he offers a constructive critique, which is necessary for the game to continue to grow.

The experiences Coach McKenzie shares in this book will intrigue you, but, more importantly, they will educate you and show you how basketball has evolved over time into "Much More than Just a Game."

Preface

I was first introduced to the game when I was seven years old; my father took me to my Uncle Stan's high school basketball game. Uncle Stan would later go on to play at NYU and ultimately in the National Basketball Association.

Like most urban youth, I too would be overtaken with the aura of the game called basketball, with hopes of playing in the NBA. I remember many days sitting on my porch in the James E. Scott projects daydreaming of the day that I would be introduced in the New York Knicks starting lineup at Madison Square Garden.

It was a dream that would never materialize; after what would be considered a decent high school career, my college career was cut short due to a bad attitude and a lack of focus. I was the player that could have never played for Coach McKenzie.

But as only God would have it, providing an opportunity for redemption, he would find a place for me to give back and impact the lives of young men who were just like me.

This book has allowed me to reflect on the many life lessons and opportunities that the game of basketball has presented me, both as a player and as a coach, including:

- Learning to appreciate the joy of victory while remaining humble, and learning how to get back up, dust myself off, and move on after the agony of defeat.

- To believe when others stop believing, and to attempt to find joy in every moment that God allows me here on earth, no matter how difficult or challenging.

- To be responsible for my own attitude and understand that I can only control me, to always be open to learning, and to know that life is about serving others so that the world might be a better place.

It has brought me lifelong friendships with those who I called Coach and those who have called me Coach, former teammates, players, and opponents.

I hope you enjoy what I shared and when you are finished you too would agree that basketball is "Much More than Just a Game."

Acknowledgments/Gratitudes

Thanks to some very important and special people in life:

- My wife, Dianne Pope McKenzie, a true blessing, you have stood by me every step of the way, in good times and in some very challenging times. I have finally completed the book, thanks to your encouragement and support. Thank you for your patience and know that you mean the world to me and are much appreciated.

- Rashida and Lawrence, I'm blessed to be your father. I thank God for each of you daily. We are extremely proud of the young adults you have become.

- My mother, Retha J. McKenzie, who tirelessly has given her love and wisdom to this family and whose personal sacrifice has kept this family together.

- Rev. Pauline Jones, the matriarch of the Jones-McKenzie family, who celebrated her one hundredth birthday last year. Since my birth you have been the wind beneath my sail. My praying grandmother who kept each of us lifted up, through you we have learned to trust in the Lord with all our heart and lean not to our own understanding, but to always acknowledge God in all we do.

- To Paula, Carla, and John, my siblings, we've come a long way since our days in the James E. Scott projects. God has truly smiled on each of us.

- My best friends, Artis Miller, Regenald Flake, and Felton Smith, all of whom I respect and admire. Each of you has brought so much value to my life in your own special way. Thanks for touching my life.

- Jules Dunbar, my little brother through Big Brothers/Big Sisters, who got me started in this coaching thing.

- To the guys that laced them up with the Wesac Magic, we had some fun times.

- Bishop Efrem Smith, my friend and pastor, who taught me a new way to coach by allowing me to join his staff at Minneapolis Patrick Henry and to the three particular players, Johnnie Gilbert, Greg Patton, and Tony Travis, who listened intently that spring day and believed in the vision for Patriot basketball.

- All of my assistant coaches, who have shared in both the celebrations and challenges of developing the lives of young men as champions in the classroom, on the hardwood, in their families, and in their communities.

- To each and every young man that I have coached over the last thirty years; they say they have been blessed by me, but I am the one that has truly been blessed.

- Last, but definitely not least, many thanks to each of you who bought this book; I hope you gain a knowledge of and appreciation for both life and the game!

Introduction

Basketball is a game that is played by nearly three hundred million people worldwide, and an estimated forty-five million in the United States. It is one of America's most popular sports but is also a very popular sport in other countries as well. Interestingly enough, it is a very culturally diverse sport and has opened up new doors all across the world, bringing foreign players to America to play the game at its highest level. Michael Jordan, the most recognized player to ever play the game of basketball, has made it an extremely popular sport. His athletic ability on the court along with his consumer appeal in advertising has broadened his image to fans across the world.

Basketball has become America's number one participatory sport. Basketball players have increased in numbers by over 25 percent in the past ten years

Even James Naismith couldn't imagine the growth of the game. Naismith was challenged by Dr. Luther Halsey Gilick Jr. to create an indoor activity as an outlet for sometimes unruly groups of students during the long, cold winter months in New England.

Naismith's challenge was to create a game that could be played indoors, would be interesting, easy to play, and could be played by artificial light. After reflecting on popular childhood games, Dr. Naismith had the school janitor nail two peach baskets to the lower rail of the gymnasium balcony, one at each end, while the school secretary typed the original thirteen rules.

With eighteen students in the class, Naismith selected two captains and had them choose sides. There were three forwards, three centers and three backs on each team; he chose two centers to jump and threw the ball up between them. It was the start of the first basketball game—the beginning of what would become a global phenomena.

The game was an immediate success, and the first game finished with a score of 1-0. The first college basketball game was played on February 9, 1895, between Hamline College and the Minnesota School of Agriculture, with Minnesota taking the game, 9–3.

Basketball slowly developed over time, and on January 18, 1896, the first college basketball game was played with the with five-man format in Iowa City, Iowa. During the game, the University of Chicago defeated the University of Iowa, 15–12.

How do you think you would do playing by these rules?

13 Rules of Basketball—Written by James Naismith

1. The ball may be thrown in any direction with one or both hands.

2. The ball may be batted in any direction with one or both hands, but never with the fist.

3. A player cannot run with the ball. The player must throw it from the spot on which he catches it, allowance to be made for a man running at good speed.

4. The ball must be held by the hands. The arms or body must not be used for holding it.

5. No shouldering, holding, pushing, striking, or tripping in any way of an opponent. The first infringement of this rule by any person shall count as a foul; the second shall disqualify him until the next goal is made or, if there was evident intent to injure the person, for the whole of the game. No substitution shall be allowed.

6. A foul is striking at the ball with the fist, violations of Rules 3 and 4 and such as described in Rule 5.

7. If either side makes three consecutive fouls it shall count as a goal for the opponents (consecutive means without the opponents in the meantime making a foul).

8. A goal shall be made when the ball is thrown or batted from the grounds into the basket and stays there, providing those defending the goal do no touch or disturb the goal. If the ball rests on the edges, and the opponent moves the basket, it shall count as a goal.

9. When the ball goes out of bounds, it shall be thrown into the field and played by the first person touching it. In case of dispute the umpire shall throw it straight into the field. The thrower-in is allowed five seconds. If he holds it longer, it shall go to the opponent. If any side persists in delaying the game, the umpire shall call a foul on them.

10. The umpire shall be the judge of the men and shall note the fouls and notify the referee when three consecutive fouls have been made. He shall have power to disqualify men according to Rule 5.

11. The referee shall be judge of the ball and shall decide when the ball is in play, in bounds, to which side it belongs, and shall keep the time. He shall decide when a goal has been made and keep account of the goals, with any other duties that are usually performed by a referee.

12. The time shall be two fifteen-minute halves, with five minutes rest between.

13. The side making the most goals in that time shall be declared the winner.

Chapter 1

Business

With all the hoopla and excitement, one topic that is often lost in the discussion of the game of basketball is its economics and the fact that it is a business. Like many of this country's early inventions, it has experienced many transformations.

As a young man growing up, basketball for me was just a game, no different from duck-duck, goose or rock, paper-scissors; it was something that brought friends together for fun and laughter. It was something that I could do alone, always imaging hitting that winning shot or free throw as the clock was winding down: five, four, three, two, one!

It was an opportunity for bonding with my dad, who always shared his old school tricks, or my younger brother, by playing one on one, and, of course, I always won.

We played two on two, three on three, four on four or five on five, always on asphalt or concrete and without adult supervision. We played half court or full court, and we organized the games and called our own fouls.

My greatest childhood memory is playing hustle, or twenty-one, as it is known today, on a dirt patch next to a train track surrounded by mulberry bushes with a bike rim nailed to a light post. That could never happen today.

It was about having fun, competing, playing hard, and just simply trying to be the best player I could be. Your reward was respect and being picked first when you returned to the court. Traveling basketball for me growing up was going from Liberty City to play a team in Overtown on Dorsey Park.

Modern basketball is played with uniforms and always in a gym with two or more courts, organized by youth sports organizations and supervised by adults, who decide when, where, and who can play.

We picked teams by the first two players making a shot from the top of the key; today teams are picked by moms and dads, who usually include their son or daughter, their kid's best friend, and three others that can afford to pay the fees.

The game that I once played for fun has blossomed into a multibillion dollar industry where kids are used like chess pieces so that adults can be crowned kings or queens.

The business of basketball includes selling sneakers, specialized training, traveling basketball, recruiting services, youth associations, and more, but it strides on selling pipe dreams through the magic of smoke screens.

The 5th Dimension used to sing, "You don't have to be a star to be in my show." Today everybody has to be the star!

Most recently I was reminded by a mom that her son was ranked as one of the top players in his class and that he averaged thirty points a game on his other team, so "if he wasn't going to be allowed to shoot when he wanted to, he wouldn't be playing anymore."

It preys on adults who live vicariously through their kids; "I didn't make it, but you will." Those whose careers were ended by that vaunted knee injury, or otherwise they would have played in the league, believe that their son or daughter is the ticket that will allow them to escape poverty or simply upgrade their lifestyle to that of the rich and famous. They believe that their son or daughter is the next Big Ticket (KG) or Candace Parker. Finally, it's a chance for them to redeem the injustice of the coach who said they couldn't play or weren't good enough, and to lay down the burden that they've had to carry over the years.

It begins with the innocent mistake of purchasing that Nerf ball and the minihoop that many of us proud fathers buy within months of our children's birth. We proudly watch and proclaim the great potential exhibited by our sons and daughters.

For me it started with the purchase of a pair of fifty-dollar Jordan shoes for my three-month-old son. It continued with anything advertised or worn by Orlando Magic and Penny Hardaway.

Like so many parents with dreams of their kids getting a free college education or playing at the highest level, we begin to invest thousands of dollars in chasing the dream. You eagerly spend money on personal training, tryouts, traveling expenses, and summer camps. But so often the return on your investment is not what was hoped for.

The business of basketball sucks us in, just like the bright lights of the big city. No matter what age or level you are playing at, make no mistake, it is all about business.

Look around your community, and you will find some type of youth sports organization or association. They operate under the premise of promoting good sportsmanship and quality athletic programs, but what they really are ,organizations run by youth sports entrepreneurs, and every entrepreneur I know is focused on market share and making a profit. Many of them have salaried staff and require membership fees.

They are the creators of pay to play, organizing leagues and tournaments or private teams, through which they generate millions of dollars. These major events become our family vacations, which generate dollars not only for the organizers but increase revenues for hotels, restaurants, and malls. It was reported that one small town in California hosting an AAU event generated a million dollar windfall, and the event sponsors made $45,000 in just tournament fees from one hundred teams.

When was the last tournament your child participated in a program that offered workshops on the ACT or SAT? Maybe it included a seminar on the ends and outs of recruiting or on how to deal with the media?

Let's really ask the question. Are these organizations about benefiting kids or about turning a profit?

But it doesn't stop there. What city or town doesn't have a gym or facility that is run by a former player or coach who also is a sports entrepreneur offering specialized training?

No doubt they realize that parents are willing to spend thousands of dollars in the pursuit of creating that superstar. They offer weekly sessions one to three times a week at a rate of twenty to one hundred dollars an hour; some willingly set up sessions for kids who really have little chance of ever being more than a recreational player.

I once witnessed a coach laughingly say to a parent that his son " was getting better," only later to describe him as his automated teller machine (ATM) and admit that the kid had about as good a chance of playing high school basketball as he did of walking on water. Of course there are some benefits in specialized training. As a coach and parent, I certainly see value in specialized training and have been fortunate to work with really good personal trainers—guys who took extreme pride in their work and cared about really helping kids get better.

But the training has to be about developing the kid's skills and not be strictly a business relationship.

But so often I have seen parents investing in training when they should be investing in a tutorial course for reading or the standardized tests. The belief is that if my child improves that jump shot or increases their vertical, that D1 scholarship will be obtained and maybe, just maybe, one day his or her name will be called in that NBA or WNBA draft.

There are three hundred D1 basketball schools, most with a rotation of no more than nine players who actually play, which totals twenty-seven hundred potential NBA draft picks. The NBA drafts only sixty players each year, with a limited number actually making the team. Your odds are just as great playing the Mega Millions or the Powerball on a weekly basis and winning as they are of playing in the NBA or WNBA.

The reality is that only two out of every one hundred high school athletes will ever play in college, and only one out of every twelve thousand high school athletes will ever become professional players.

Because specialized training has a small profit margin, many of these facilities sponsor traveling teams. How can we talk about the business of basketball without discussing traveling, AAU, and grassroots basketball?

Traveling basketball is the trap that has parents believing that if their kids don't start playing at four or five years old they will fall behind their peers. It's pay to play basketball, writing a check so that my kid can be on a team, and you are darn right I expect him or her to play!

People confuse AAU basketball with grassroots basketball; the Amateur Athletic Union (AAU) is one of the largest sports nonprofit organizations in the United States. Founded in 1888 with the purpose to establish standards and uniformity in amateur sports, it administers thirty-two different sports. However, it is estimated that 50 percent or more of its more than 1.1 million members participate in basketball. Although it encourages participation at an early age, with the AAU national championships starting at eight and under, the AAU attempts to regulate teams through its national office, sanctioning all AAU basketball teams and events. Proof of grade and membership are required.

So while people refer to the summer basketball circuit, or circus, as "AAU basketball," only a small percentage of the summer events are actually sponsored or affiliated with the AAU.

Grassroots basketball, now that's a horse of a different color. For the majority of high school coaches, it's their worst nightmare. It has as much regulation as a dogfight in a dark alley. It has been described as being much like the subprime mortgage market, making up the rules as they go along, and always in the interest of making a dollar. In 2006 at an NBA finals press conference, Commissioner David Stern described it as exploitation of amateurs and perpetuation of poor fundamentals. The former NCAA president, Myles Brand, describes it as the dysfunctional world of youth basketball.

At the heart of grassroots basketball is the shoe war. Basketball historians credit or blame (you can choose for yourself) Sonny Vacaro, the former Nike, Adidas, and Reebok shoe executive.

In my era Chuck Taylor's was the shoe of the trade. If you played the game of basketball you wore Converse; that changed in 1984 when Sonny Vacaro signed the then twenty-one-year-old NBA rookie Michael Jordan to an endorsement deal. It began the declaration of war amongst the sneaker companies as they all began pursuit of the next Jordan.

It was Vacaro who revolutionized the game by paying college coaches to use Nikes as their team shoe, later adding team gear. He was the first shoe executive to pay grassroots and high school coaches money that sometimes reached six figures, and he is the creator of the now popular elite basketball camps.

TV analyst Len Elmore, who played college and professional basketball, graduated from Harvard, and is now the executive of Ihoops, has been quoted as saying "that shoe companies' spending has thrown youth basketball into turmoil."

Vacaro refutes his critics, saying, "No matter which shoe company I've worked with, I've never said we weren't in business to make money."

Others say that the NCAA should share the blame for what happens with grassroots basketball because of its restructuring the recruiting calendar and putting emphasis on summer basketball over traditional high school.

Grassroots basketball is certainly a hot topic amongst high school coaches. The question of who really has the player's best interest at heart and who works at developing his skills creates a real tug of war between high school coaches and grassroots coaches. Many believe that AAU and grassroots basketball are ruining the game by emphasizing an individualistic style of play.

Its run-and-gun style of play is in complete opposition to concepts of offense and defense emphasized by the high school coach.

Michael Hyde, of St. Andrew's School (Middleton, Delaware) is quoted in *Winning Hoops* magazine as saying:

"It is a fact that for most elite players, summer basketball has become more important than their high school team. Grassroots coaches are viewed as having more influence than the high school coaches. Some assistant say that recruiting elite talent would be almost impossible without strong ties to grassroots programs".

Back in the day, as the kids say, high school coaches used to have a relationship with their players, and they were seen as the gatekeepers. It's been awhile, but I made it a habit to be involved with my players' recruitment along with their parents. However, in the ten years I've been coaching, that has changed.

Parents, particularly single mothers, seem to be mesmerized by the charm of dashing young men who could sell sand on a beach, and really believe these programs have their kids' best interest at heart. Players today have street agents and large posses that influence their decisions—people pulling them in all kinds of directions.

I constantly told my players that they really needed to assess even those that really love them; which of course is a difficult challenge for kids. As a smart athlete you must be willing to ask yourself this questions: Do those claiming to care really have my best interest at heart?

No matter who you want to blame, there is plenty of blame to go around. When P. T. Barnum proclaimed, "There is a sucker born every minute," who knew it would one day pertain to those in pursuit of basketball?

While grassroots basketball benefits the top-tier basketball players, it's the ones who have no chance of being in that top 3 percent that goes on to play college ball who are being sold pipe dreams.

Every season I watch the top grassroots coaches and program directors as they attend high school games like major college scouts trying to find the next John Wall. Some are respectful enough to make sure coaches are aware of their interest in a certain kid, while others have no regard for the coach or the fact that the team still has half of its season left to play.

Summer basketball is really spring ball, as tryouts are held when the final whistle is blown for the winter basketball season. Kids and parents excited about being called elite are usually charged for the opportunity to wear snazzy uniforms and to "get exposure," which I find interesting, since the NCAA has almost eliminated the April recruiting period, allowing a minimal number of days out, and for the most part coaches are not allowed out until the July recruiting period.

Most but not all tryouts are shams, because most of the time the teams already know who they intend to keep and who doesn't have a chance. They have recruited who they wanted.

The best kids usually play for free, and others pay thousands to finance the team with hopes of being seen by North Carolina, Kentucky, or Duke. One of the funniest stories I heard was from a parent whose son was on a team with some very elite talent, players who no question were the type that big-time programs would be recruiting. He bragged that Bill Self, Roy Williams, and other top-tier coaches had been in the audience to see his son. His son was on the team with four top one hundred players. Who do you really think they were there to see? But parents are foolish enough to believe that if their kid plays on an elite grassroots team, they are guaranteed to play D1 or in the NBA.

How about parents who travel the country with sixth-grade teams for exposure? What college coach whose son or daughter is not playing wants the assignment of evaluating sixth-graders?

You think Eminem could have possibly been thinking about grassroots hoops when he wrote the real *Slim Shady*? It does seem to have its seedy characters, scams, and scandals. You hear stories of guys like Myron Piggie, the legendary Nike grassroots operator who gave thousands of dollars to kids in the St. Louis area, or the Wisconsin operator that happens to run a scouting service on the side, charging kids to be ranked.

Its by-products include stories like O. J. Mayo, who some say started receiving money from agents as a seventh-grader, and Renardo Sidney, who at one time was thought to be the best player in his class and future number one draft pick of the NBA. He played for three high schools and three summer teams in two states. His dad, Renardo Sr., was paid $20,000 a year as a Reebok "consultant." He also coached the LA Dream Team, sponsored by Reebok. Clark Francis wrote, "Sidney could be the poster boy for the things that are wrong with grassroots basketball and is the perfect example of just how bad the sense of entitlement among many of these players has become."

There are always stories about the shady coaches who become the personal advisors, pretending that they've got the back of the potential superstar, but when the opportunity presents itself, they capitalize, cha-ching. There are guys like Pat Barret, who allegedly was paid $250,000 to deliver Kevin Love to a well-known sports agency.

You can't discuss the business of basketball without including college basketball; it's the catalyst behind much of the madness that doesn't start in March. Who's foolish enough to believe it's amateur sports? The players may not get paid, but everybody else does.

College basketball is big business. It's about nice arenas, whose naming rights are sold to major corporations, with luxury suites for them to entertain their clients. It's megamillion-dollar coaching contracts and selling sports apparel in team colors.

In 2006, Bill Thomas, then chairman of the House Ways and Means Committee, wrote a letter to then NCAA President Myles Brand.

Thomas said, "The annual return also states that one of the NCAA's purposes is to retain a clear line of demarcation between intercollegiate athletics and professional sports. Corporate sponsorships, multimillion dollar television deals, highly paid coaches with no academic duties and dedication of inordinate amounts of time by athletes to training lead many to believe that major college football and men's basketball more closely resemble professional sports than amateur sports."

To call college basketball amateur sports is like calling Mount Rushmore a hill. Corporations pay as much as $100,000 for a thirty-second ad during the early rounds of the NCAA tournament. The NCAA television deal is worth $ 6.1 billion over eleven years for TV rights.

If one was to divide the $548 million made by the NCAA during last year's March madness amongst the sixty-five teams, each of the twelve players would get a check in the amount of $670,000, and this doesn't take into account any ticket sales, merchandise, concessions, or proceeds from the regular season.

Some argue, "What's the big deal? These kids are getting a free education." But are they really?

Every year during the NCAA tournament, Richard Lapchick of Diversity and Ethics in Sports (TIDES) at the University of Central Florida releases the graduation rates of the participating teams in "Keeping Score When It Counts." Last year his study found that 64 percent of the teams participating in the NCAA tournament graduated 50 percent of all its players, but the percentage of graduation for African-American differed by 31 percent.

At the end of the 2009 basketball season, the NBA and NCAA created the Youth Basketball Initiative, aimed at addressing the challenges of grassroots basketball. AAU President Bobby Dodd said that a representative of the Amateur Athletic Union attended a couple of meetings, but there was little interest in their organization. When told that only a couple of meetings had been held, Chuck Daley said simply, "Follow the money."

In the end, it's about winning. Winning requires that you have the best players; the best players sell tickets and sponsorships, which make the alumni proud. Proud, successful alumni become big-time program boosters. Big-time program boosters make sure coaches have what they need to be successful, if you know what I mean.

Bryan Crawford makes it clear in his article "Corruption in Amateur Athletics," (August 2009): Slam Magazine

> The NCAA is in bed with shoe companies who provide revenue in exchange for sponsorships of their programs. The Amateur Athletic Union is also in bed with the shoe companies who sponsor them. AAU coaches then get in bed with the shoe companies who sponsor and outfit their programs and give them all expenses paid trips to their biggest AAU tournaments. College coaches, already in bed with shoe companies by default, go to these tournaments scouting players and find themselves in bed with AAU coaches in order to get the inside track on signing a kid. In some cases even paying to have these kids delivered to them. And with all these people in bed together you know what happens? Somebody's getting screwed. And it's almost always the kid.

So next time you lace them up, ask yourself, are you the player or you getting played?

WESAC Magic Photo

Chapter 2

Appreciate

We spend so much of our lives chasing dreams, trying to capture the desires of our heart, with very little time spent appreciating our creator's blessings.

Most of us go about our daily business with little or no thoughts of thanks or appreciation for all those special people who have touched our lives.

You don't appreciate your health until you get sick; you can't appreciate being rich until you know what it's like to have been poor. You don't appreciate true love until you've experienced heartbreak.

You get the picture. As the old saying goes, you don't appreciate what you've got until it's gone. The same goes for the people in our lives.

A couple of years ago I lost my father, and while I was fortunate to spend some very memorable moments with him, I often find myself thinking about the things we didn't get a chance to do.

When was the last time you thanked those special people who have touched your life and told them how much you have appreciated what they've done? I mean besides Thanksgiving, the one day a year that we take time to at least consciously reflect on our blessings.

An unknown author once penned the thought, "No one who

achieves success does so without acknowledging the help of others. The wise and confident acknowledge the help with appreciation."

On your quest to pursuing stardom in your basketball career, having fun and happiness should be among your top priorities. Learning to appreciate life and the people, places, and things in it is a very big aspect of that.

In order to be successful you have to learn how to appreciate both pleasant and even seemingly unpleasant experiences. Why? Because as human beings we take things for granted, even life itself. Think about it; your body functions through no effort of yours. You breathe, your heart beats, your organs do their thing nonstop, and you wake up in the morning. And we get up and go on about our daily lives without acknowledging that; that is, until something happens.

Take time to appreciate the opportunities that this game will bring you, the places that you will travel, and the lifelong friendships that you will establish.

My wife and I were blessed in 2006 to travel to South Africa and, in particular, Botswana, with Athletes in Action, as part the sports ministry team. We actually celebrated our twenty-fifth wedding anniversary on this trip.

It was a life-changing experience for a number of reasons, but most importantly because it made me appreciate just how blessed I was to live in a great country like the United States, and, in spite of its shortcomings, America is still the best country in the world.

It made me appreciate how fortunate I was, as I witnessed orphans infected with HIV and kids looking in trashcans for their next meals.

I met a great young Christian pastor, Gary Pelotshweu, who I continue to communicate with and plan on assisting with building a school to be used by young kids.

You should appreciate the thrill of victory and the agony of defeat and all the lessons that will be learned in between.

Appreciate the opportunity to represent your school at whatever level; it's a privilege, not a right. You should be honored to represent your communities and to have hundreds, sometimes thousands, cheer for you!

Be thankful for a coach that will settle for nothing less than your best, a coach with passion and love for the game, who truly understands that the game of life is the most important game you'll ever play.

No matter what's your final destination with this game of basketball, many will touch your life on the journey, some up close and some from a distance. They will give, and you will take the sacrifices they make, and for many of you the sacrifices will be numerous.

So while you chase your dreams don't forget to thank those people who help you along the way.

Your Parents

Take it from a parent who knows all too well what it means to sacrifice for his children's dreams. For twenty years, my wife and I willfully gave our time and money for our kids to pursue their love of basketball. Our schedules, meals, and vacations revolved around the kids' practices, games, and traveling to and from weekend tournaments. With two kids, we sometimes passed like two ships in the night while traveling to opposite sides of the city.

Sometimes the money we set aside for our personal desires went to AAU fees or assuring that they both had the "flyest kicks" (their words, not mine). The more success they achieved, the more sacrifices we made. Nationals for boys and girls are rarely, if ever, held at the same time in the same state, and, of course, one of us always had to travel with them.

As a result, my golf game never quite took off because I spent more time in the gym than on the course, but I digress. We never complained. Oh, the things parents do for love … and basketball!

Kids don't understand the sacrifices that parents make so that they can have the opportunities that they have. I certainly didn't.

Your Coaches

I personally never imagined myself ever being a coach; the one thing in life I knew that I didn't want to do was work with kids. Obviously, God had a different plan, and I've been tapped on the shoulder to make a difference in the lives of young women and men.

You should know that coaching is no easy task. You're judged by the final score on the scoreboard, and everybody watching in the stands always thinks they're a better coach than you are.

The expectations are sometimes unrealistic. In watching one of my favorite movies, *Remember the Titans*, I recall Coach Boone warning the community, when being introduced as their new football coach, "I'm not Martin Luther King, Jesus Christ, or the Easter bunny." While coaches may not be any of that, they are mentors, surrogate fathers, teachers, and chauffeurs, to name a few.

Coaches are required to be real models and not role models, as we are entrusted with not only developing the talents but the lives of those who come to us as girls and boys and leave as young men and women. It means that you must be willing to give your time, talents, and monies.

Back when my daughter was playing AAU, and I coached her team, we qualified for Nationals in Memphis, Tennessee. The girls were thrilled but, at the same time, sad because we had no way to get there. It was an inner-city squad, full of talent but short on cash and opportunity. We had to go. You know, Nationals is a big deal. That's where you get a chance to showcase your skills in front of scouts from all over. It's maybe the only shot some kids get at playing on the next level.

So, eleven of us packed into my wife's minivan and drove about thirteen hours to Memphis, Tennessee, and it was no picnic. Nine girls plus two coaches in a seven-passenger van with luggage equals a pretty crowded ride. Due to our lack of funds, I made arrangements for us to stay in a local dormitory.

We couldn't afford a hotel, although it did seem like a motel—a roach motel, that is!

Although, we didn't win the tournament, the trip wasn't a total loss. I took the girls to talk to the coach at the University of Memphis so they could see in person what their dream would look like if they continued to pursue it. We also visited several historical sites, including the National Civil Rights Museum, where they sat on a replica of the Montgomery bus that Rosa Parks refused to give up her seat on. We also toured the Lorraine Motel, where Dr. Martin Luther King was assassinated, and a house turned museum that the slaves used in the Underground Railroad. It was a life-changing experience for me, and one that I know those girls will never forget. In addition to that, some girls, including my daughter, got letters from interested colleges. So for me the trip was well worth it.

John Wooden says that coaches don't really know whether or not they have done a good job until ten years after your kids have left; it takes that long for them to figure it out.

Your Teachers

While a teacher has the responsibility for inspiring and molding the minds of our children, they are probably the least appreciated. They too are overworked and underpaid.

Teaching is an occupation that finds its rewards in being difference makers; it certainly has nothing to do with a big paycheck.

Teachers are often looked upon as the enemy, yet they are the ones who have dedicated their lives to developing and shaping your life in hopes that you will achieve your dream.

They are the ones who made you the expert in the subject and also have been the motivational factor behind your success. For some students, a teacher may be the only adult that listens to them and responds, whether they are right or wrong. As students, we often fail to acknowledge the contribution of our teachers until much later in life.

So, if given a chance, don't forget to recognize and appreciate the efforts a teacher puts into giving your life direction.

You can be a happy person, but until you take the time to appreciate what you have and the people that help you get there, you will never reach your greatest potential, personally or professionally.

**Larry and Dianne 25th wedding anniversary on
Athletes In Action Mission Trip to Africa**

Chapter 3

Student-Athlete

The game has changed in so many ways, and today the dream for almost every parent and every boy and girl who's playing is to earn a basketball scholarship.

For some the dream does come true, but really it's only the chosen few.

Young people and their parents spend thousands of dollars investing in their kids traveling across the country playing games, trying to improve their ball handling, hoping they develop a jumpshot, or trying to increase their vertical.

As a coach it's both laughable and frustrating to see the emphasis parents put on how many points their kid scored, with little interest in whether the team won or lost.

In all of my years of coaching, what I've found is that the most important statistic is seldom discussed because it's not found in the weekly sports section. I sometimes wonder how many parents would stick their chest out if their kid's grade point average was next to their points per game.

My experience as a coach who has had numerous kids recruited is that not once can I recall being asked about how many points or rebounds my kids averaged. Coaches always were concerned about work ethic, character, and whether they were coachable. Being that student-athlete is crucial to giving yourself a chance to being recruited and playing at the next level.

According to the NCAA document *Estimated Probability of Competing in Athletics Beyond the High School Interscholastic Level,* 546,335 young men participated in high school basketball and 452,929 young ladies participated. November 2010

Of the boys playing high school basketball, 156,096 were seniors, and for girls 129,408 were seniors. There is a 3 percent chance of each ever playing college basketball.

There are only 329 Division I and 290 Division II colleges that offer men's basketball scholarships. There are 328 Division I and 291 Division II colleges that offer women scholarships.

That means a total of 7,177 men's basketball scholarships are available for NCAA schools; 9,285 are available for women. Some NAIA schools do offer scholarships too, but not all scholarships are full scholarships. Sometimes a partial scholarship is combined with a student grant-in-aid.

The simple fact is that the odds are not in the average high school player's favor. As I discussed earlier, college basketball is a business, and a scholarship is an investment.

In March 2011, *USA Today* published an article that determined that the total value of participating at the Division I level was worth $120,000 annually. This includes a median scholarship value of $27,923.

The scholarship includes tuition, room and board, and other fees, but players are rewarded by receiving some of the great coaching, medical care, first-class treatment for injuries, trips to exotic locations during the winter, free tickets, media relations, and hopefully one day a very good job.

With the challenge of schools meeting the requirements of the academic performance rate, schools have to be relatively sure that you are a good investment.

College coaches can't invest in marginal students because their athletic programs could be penalized for their players failing to take care of business in the classroom.

Student-athletes who become academically ineligible, transfer, decide to turn pro, or don't graduate can cause the team to lose points under the APR, which leads to the loss of scholarships, which leads to loss of tickets sold, and which leads eventually to a coach losing his or her job.

One of the real challenges for young players and parents is that all too often high school coaches are really unfamiliar with the recruiting process and its requirements.

So here are a few tips

All students who's desire to compete at the Division I level are now required to complete and be evaluated on sixteen core courses.

Core means that you are taking four years of English, three years of math (algebra or higher), two years of natural/physical science (one year of lab if offered at your high school), one year of additional English, mathematics, or natural physical science, two years of social science, and four years of additional courses (from any of those previously mentioned, foreign language, or nondoctrinal religion/philosophy).

In Division II, there is no sliding scale. The minimum grade point average is 2.000.The minimum SAT score is 820 (verbal and math sections only) and the minimum ACT sum score is 68.

If there's one thing to take from here, it is that you shouldn't put all your eggs in one basket. If parents are looking for financial assistance, they should be aware that it's been estimated that there are thirty times more scholarship dollars available for college academic scholarships than there are for athletic scholarships. While it is a dream for young athletes and parents to earn an athletic scholarship, you must keep things in perspective. The higher the grade point average, the more opportunities exist to have a scholarship offered.

NCAA DIVISION I MEN'S BASKETBALL OFF-CAMPUS RECRUITING GUIDE

Effective August 1, 2008

Freshman/Sophomore Junior Senior Two-Year College Prospects Four-Year College Prospects Evaluations and Contacts

Recruiting materials -

☐ June 15 following
sophomore year.
Telephone calls -

☐ Once per month
beginning June 15
following sophomore
year.
Telephone calls -

☐ One per month
through July 31.
Telephone calls -

☐ Twice per week
beginning
August 1.
Off-campus contact -

☐ September 9.
Official visit -

☐ Opening day of
prospect's classes.
Telephone calls -

☐ Once per week.
Qualifier -

☐ Contacts permissible.
Nonqualifier -

☐ No contacts until after
completion of first year of
enrollment at the two-year
college.
Official visits -

☐ Maximum of five beginning
October 15 following
prospect's completion of high
school.
Telephone calls -

☐ Once per week following permission.
NCAA or NAIA institution -

☐ Only after written permission has
been granted by the student-athlete's
institution.
Other four-year institution -

☐ Written permission not necessary.
Official visits -

☐ Maximum of five beginning October 15 following prospect's completion of high school.

☐ 130 recruiting-person days during academic year evaluation periods.

☐ Not more than seven recruiting opportunities (contacts and evaluations combined) during the academic year per prospect.

☐ Not more than three off-campus contacts during prospect's senior year.

☐ No off-campus contacts during junior year.

☐ Practice/competition site restrictions (see other side).

*Please note that this document should not be used as a substitute for the NCAA manual. Coaches are encouraged to contact the athletics compliance office for additional information.

DEFINITIONS

Contact

A contact is any face-to-face encounter between a prospect or the prospect's parents, relatives or legal guardian(s) and an institutional staff member or athletics representative during which any dialogue occurs in excess of an exchange of a greeting. Any such face-to-face encounter that is prearranged (e.g., positions himself/herself in a location where contact is possible) or that takes place on the grounds of the prospect's educational institution or at the site of organized competition or practice involving the prospect or the prospect's high school, preparatory school, two-year college or all-star team shall be considered a contact, regardless of whether any conversation occurs. However, an institutional staff member or athletics representative who is approached by a prospect or the prospect's parents, relatives or legal guardian(s) at any location shall not use a contact, provided the encounter was not prearranged and the staff member or athletics representative does not engage in any dialogue in excess of a greeting and takes appropriate steps to immediately terminate the encounter.

Evaluation

Evaluation is any off-campus activity designed to assess the academic qualifications or athletics ability of a prospect, including any visit to a prospect's educational institution (during which no contact occurs) or the observation of a prospect participating in any practice or competition at any site.

Recruiting-Person Days -- Men's Basketball

A recruiting-person day is defined as one coach engaged in an off-campus recruiting activity of prospect on one day (12:01 a.m. to midnight); two coaches engaged in recruiting activities on the same day shall use two recruiting person days.

Recruited Prospective Student-Athlete

Actions by staff members or athletics representatives that cause a prospect to become a recruited prospect at that institution are:

a. Providing the prospect with an official visit;
b. Having an arranged, in-person, off-campus encounter with the prospect or the prospect's parent(s), relatives or legal guardian(s);
c. Initiating or arranging a telephone contact with the prospect, the prospect's relatives or legal guardian(s) on more than one occasion for the purpose of recruitment; and
d. Issuing a National Letter of Intent or the institution's written offer of athletically related financial aid to the prospect (excluding summer term awards prior to initial full-time enrollment).

Telephone Calls

All electronically transmitted human voice exchange (including videoconferencing and videophones) shall be considered telephone calls. All electronically transmitted correspondence (e.g., electronic mail, facsimiles) shall not be considered telephone calls.

Contacts, Evaluations and Telephone Calls
Off-Campus Recruiters

An institutional staff member is not permitted to recruit off campus until he or she has been certified on an annual basis as to knowledge of applicable recruiting rules.

Telephone Calls During Conduct of Athletics Contest

Telephone calls to a prospect [or the prospect's relatives or legal guardian(s)] may not be made during the conduct of any of the institution's intercollegiate athletics contests in that sport until the competition has concluded and the team has been dismissed by the coach.

Telephone Calls - Institutional Staff Members -- General Rule

All telephone calls to prospects (or the prospects' parents, legal guardians or coaches) must be made by the head coach or one or more of the assistant coaches who count toward the numerical limitations in men's basketball.

Visits to a Prospect's Educational Institution

Institutional staff members may visit a prospect's educational institution on not more than one occasion during a particular week within a contact or evaluation period, regardless of the number of prospects enrolled in the institution or whether any prospect is contacted on that occasion. During the July evaluation period, there are no limitations on the number of times an institutional staff member may visit a prospect's educational institution.

In the end, academics should always be your priority because when you have played your last game it's the educated students who would be the ultimate winners.

Rashida McKenzie
Academic All-Conference
Norfolk State University

Chapter 4

Knowledge of the Game

Quick, what was the name of the man that invented the game of basketball?

A) Michael Jordan
B) James Naismith
C) Larry Bird

The answer is (B). Dr. James Naismith invented the game of basketball in 1891. Believe it or not, when I ask that question, some of the kids I've worked with over the years have answered (A) Michael Jordan, who didn't even lace up a pair of sneakers until almost eighty years later. Sadly, those kids are probably just as likely to practice more on a Playstation, Xbox or Wii than they are in a gym. Why is this significant? Because although basketball may arguably be the most popular team sport in the universe, so few that play the game have a true knowledge of the game.

Somewhere in basketball travels I read, "The game is just a game, unless you have knowledge of the game."

Very little time is spent watching the game, and call me old school, but kids these days aren't really fans of the game. They're fans of some of the players in the game: Lebron, Kobe, Dwayne Wade, KG—the big names. If you can't name the sixth man on the roster of any of the players listed above, then I rest my case. What makes each of these players the standouts that they have become is their court awareness, the ability to read the defense, and the elevated skill level that allows them to navigate the floor with ease. The only way to become that good and gain knowledge of the game is to become a student of the game.

Being a student of the game raises your level of performance. It allows you to be able to add something special to your game—the "IT" factor that makes you stand out! It's about finding a way to excel in the game beyond what is on the stat sheet.

Some would say that Kobe Bryant is the best player to play the game of basketball, past and present, comparing him only to great basketball legend Michael Jordan. In an article in the *Los Angeles Times*, Kobe Bryant's greatness is attributed to his dedication to excelling just as much off the court as he does on the court. It is said that no player or coach spends more time studying his opponents than Kobe Bryant. Before every game you will find him with a portable DVD player watching clips of the players he'll be guarding that particular game. He's looking for just the slightest advantage. He knows that every player has habits, certain tendencies. He's watching to see if they've added a new move. Are they driving aggressively to the basket, or are they settling for the jump shot? That way when the time comes he can take them out of their comfort zone. He's been intently analyzing the game like this since he was six years old.

Although kids are starting to play organized basketball in second and third grade, there's more emphasis on running plays and being crowned champion in the weekend tournament than on learning the basic fundamentals. Summertime used to be spent working on their game and trying to get better, but with the emergence of AAU and fall leagues, winter leagues and regular season games, when is there time to improve, time to evaluate your strengths and weaknesses? If you "wanna be like Mike," then you have to know what Mike did to get where he got.

If you're playing and competing in leagues and tournaments all year long, where is the opportunity to work on your basketball skills? The off-season is the time to develop your skills without focusing on results.

Basketball is no different from other things in life; you must understand the basics before you can master anything.

Try teaching someone to read without teaching them their alphabets, or math without understanding numbers or how to count.

The greatest players are the ones who have mastered the most basic skills. We have begun to see more and more European players being drafted into the NBA and the expansion of the league overseas primarily because of their style of game.

When I say style, I don't mean the young, fly, and flashy approach that was brought on by the streetball movement. When AND1 (the ultimate version of street basketball) became hot, the basic fundamentals were abandoned. Fascinated with the new movement, many players' focus shifted from learning the basic crossover to mastering the killing crossover, no-look passes, and taking fifteen moves to make a simple layup. The aftermath of the popular league left a generation of young athletes struggling with a basic right- or left-hand layup and turning the pick-and-roll into a move seen on *Dancing with the Stars*.

Although AND1 was very entertaining to watch, not many of those players successfully transitioned to the next level. AND1 is for show, not for those who want to go pro. If you want to mimic a style, look at the European leagues, whose players have a flair for the fundamentals. They have some of the best players because they've gone back to the basics.

Coach Randy Brown, a former college coach at Iowa State, amongst other, suggests that kids need to learn forty basic basketball skills. These skills should be semi-mastered before attempting to try out for a high school team.

40
Skill Development Checklist

1. Stance
2. Balance
3. Pivoting—4 uses of the pivot
4. Court Vision
5. Getting Open
6. Change of Speed
7. Change of Direction
8. Decision Making
9. Jump Stop
10. Triple Threat Position
11. Catching the Ball—Stationary
12. Catching the Ball—On the Move
13. Passing the Ball—Stationary
14. Passing the Ball—On the Move
15. Dribbling—Stationary
16. Dribbling—On the Move—Push ball in front, no holster
17. Defensive Rebounding—Head under body, no reach.
18. Offensive Rebounding
19. Form Shooting
20. Catch and Shoot—Cutting to and sliding away from ball
21. Dribble and Shoot
22. Layup
23. Scoring in the Post
24. Screening Away from the Ball
25. Screening on the Ball
26. Cutting Away From the Ball—Run through the ball
27. Defensive Stance
28. On Ball Defense
29. Help Side Defense

Those who haven't mastered the basic skills usually don't have the ability to "think outside the ball." Their capability to make something happen without having the ball in their hands is little to none. However, once you master the basic skills, then your game has unlimited potential. The best players aren't associated with one position. Kobe is just good; he's not a good guard or forward. He's good, period. He has the ability to shoot, take you to the basket, pull up, and post up. Because he can play each position, he can recognize each of them on the floor.

Well, I don't think we can discuss knowledge of the game without talking about positions, another example of how the game has changed. Every kid that plays is a point guard or small forward and must have the ball in their hands. Playing with your back to the basket is a lost art, so no one is a post player.

In the final analysis, my opinion is that there are only two positions in the game of basketball, those being perimeter and post, and everybody should be able to play and defend both. But, really, what do I know?

Let's give a brief breakdown of each position, as you know the game:

The Backcourt

#1—The point guard is one of the main basketball positions and is the leader on the floor. They must have great ballhandling skills and keep their composure under defensive pressure. They should also have pretty good shooting skills and should be able to hand out assists (which is their main job).

#2—The shooting guard should also be able to handle the ball and is the team's best shooter. They should have the ability to find their teammates that are screening to get open shots and be able to score off the dribble.

The Frontcourt

#3—The small/shooting forward is the most versatile player on the team, with the ability to hit open shots. They are a decent ball handler, and their strength is usually driving to the basket.

#4—The power forward's role is similar to the center's role. They can play low post or high post, but they have the ability to hit fifteen-foot jump shots. They understand how to set screens to get themselves and teammates open and aggressively fight for position to get offensive and defensive rebounds.

#5—The center is your big man on the floor. Their strength lies in using their size to score with their back to the basket. They also have many other important roles, such as gathering most of the rebounds.

As a student of the game, you should think of yourself as clay. The more you learn, the more likely it is for you to become an amazing "sculpture"—a one of a kind player. This can only happen if you allow the knowledge from coaches, film sessions, and books to "mold" you. You must develop the desire to not only excel on the court, but off of it too. Your team benefits from your knowledge, hence the importance of truly understanding your role. When everyone on the floor knows their role, the offense and defense runs like a well-oiled machine, a championship team machine! This is where the fun begins.

Tip-off time:
- Study your favorite player at each position.
- Learn to play more than one position; a good player doesn't limit himself.
- Research the top five basketball greats of all time.
- Read the biography of one of those greats.

Another Basketball Quiz

1. Who are the big three?
   A. Michael Jordan, Scottie Pippen, and Dennis Rodman
   B. Karl Malone, John Stockton, and Jeff Hornacek
   C. Kevin Garnett, Paul Pierce, and Ray Allen
   D. All of the above

2. Who has the most NBA championship rings?
   A. Magic Johnson
   B. Bill Russell
   C. Larry Bird
   D. Charles Barkley

Coach McKenzie teaching at Clyde Turner's Basketball Camp

Chapter 5

Enjoy

This game has become so much about parents, programs, and coaches. Some parents continue to try to live vicariously through their kids; programs are constantly seeking to one up each other, and some coaches are driven to win at all cost.

The passion for the sport of basketball quickly becomes pressure to uphold the family name. It's not okay to just play or be on the team; you must start.

It's not okay to be a starter; you need to score. It's not okay to just score; you must be the leading scorer, and not just the leading scorer, but also the all-time leading scorer.

You read story of kids like Grady Green and his mother, Daphne. Green attended eight high schools, a prep school, and two junior colleges, and finally he settled at Prairie View A&M.

While mom would say that circumstances dictated her moves, many of her son's former coaches say that it was her obsession with her son obtaining a high major scholarship and then jumping to the NBA.

By the time some kids reach high school, a lot of them are burnt out and have lost their lust for the game and forgotten what attracted them to it in the first place: *fun*! I've always believed that the game should be fun, and I remind my players to have fun prior to taking the floor.

I believe in working hard and striving to be the best that you can be, but it should be enjoyable.

Jim Hayford, one of the winningest active coaches in all of NCAA Division III basketball, says, "The purpose of youth and high school sports is: learning teamwork, enjoying sport, handling competition, enhancing friendships, accepting responsibility, and many other great developmental activities. The memories made in high school sports will last for a lifetime and are cherished as one of the best reminders of youth. When the focus becomes personal success for future achievement the big advantages of playing the team sport of basketball are lost."

It seems as though these days kids are being encouraged to start their careers at five and six years old. By the time they go to high school they have already played in roughly five hundred competitive games, all in the name of being the next Kobe or Lebron.

It is so rare to drive through the neighborhood and see kids enjoying a pick-up game; it is in danger of extinction. Everything is so structured, with adults always being in charge, and what kid enjoys adults always being present? Adults want to win, and kids want to play; adults want to be in charge, and kids want freedom. Let kids be kids. Sometimes we forget how to do that. Don't get so caught up in the score that you forget to see the world and the game the way kids do. We should try to see it that way more often.

To the Kids

Even though it's been a very long time, I can remember being fifteen years old and thinking that I couldn't wait to be grown, out of my parents' house and on my own.

Like most teens, I wanted to do what I wanted to do, when I wanted to do it! Why did my parents need to know every place I went, where I was, or who I was with?

Boy, if I had known then what I know now, I definitely would not have been in such a hurry to grow up. Being an adult comes with responsibilities. I encourage you to take the time to enjoy each step that it takes to get to adulthood. Take the time to be a child. You should enjoy hanging out with friends, riding bikes, playing tag—things that have become foreign to today's youth.

The things that you are in a hurry to get to now will always be there. You will never get too old to find a club or bar, the opposite sex won't disappear, someone will always be celebrating something, and invitations to parties will come. Automakers will continue to produce faster cars and more futuristic models. Fashion might change, but the style always comes back. My grandma used to say, "There is nothing new under the sun." She was right!

Enjoy not being concerned about the roof over your head or food on the table. Enjoy being chauffeured around and the adults in your life operating around your schedule. Enjoy the unlimited texting and phone calls, watching the costly cable, and having access to the Internet, without knowing the cost.

Jay-Z didn't drop *Reasonable Doubt* , his debut album until he was twenty-seven. He understood that while the world is a rush, true greatness takes time! That album went platinum and has been ranked by Rolling Stone as one of the 500 greatest albums of all time.

To Parents

I speak from years of experience when I say I can promise you that the costs associated with parenthood, and they are numerous, are well worth it. Like many of you, the McKenzies' was, and still is, in some respect, a basketball family. It's been a long family tradition that started with my father, Lawrence, learning the game on the streets of Miami. He became a star at Booker T. Washington High School and later in the Air Force. Since then almost every male and some of the females have engaged in the sport, some with success; others were not so successful.

Both my son and daughter followed the family tradition and started at an early age. Lawrence was fascinated with the game from birth, it seems; if you ask Rashida she'll say she was tricked into it.

One Christmas break early into our careers, Dianne and I both had to work, and we needed somewhere for the kids to go during the day.

Every year, Clyde Turner, my friend and mentor, hosted his annual Kwanza basketball camp, and it happened to be a full-day camp, a perfect solution to our problem. Against her will, Rashida attended basketball camp with her brother for the week.

Being five feet seven as a fourth grader made her a pretty popular camper. By the week's end she had fallen in love with a game that she would use until she couldn't use it anymore.

Her new passion for the game of basketball kept her busy over the next few years, playing traveling ball for a few teams, four years of high school, and three years of college before deciding that the WNBA was not in her future, and she decided to continue her involvement with the game by becoming one of the team's broadcasters. Through the game she even managed to find her prince; KO, as we call him, is a former basketball star at Norfolk State, where they both played. I even coached him during our brief stint in pursuit of professional basketball careers. They got married in September of 2009.

My son, Lawrence, started early with a house league at the YMCA. He quickly moved on to park board and then the traveling circuit. Of course the fondest memories are our days as father and son at Minneapolis Patrick Henry, where we had a nice run, winning 113 games with twelve losses, and winning four straight state titles in class AAA basketball. He went on to play at Oklahoma and later transferred to the University of Minnesota. Lawrence is still pursuing his dream to play in the NBA, l playing professionally in Macedonia and for the Los Angeles Defenders of the NBDL until his recent injury. Lawrence is the father of our first grandchild, Kailah Rae McKenzie, who probably pursue the game of basketball if my son has his way

So as I'm sure you have gathered by now, we spent lots of time and money traveling all over the country; we spent almost every weekend in a gym, but these days basketball is an afterthought for the McKenzies. The shot that was missed in fourth grade or the free throws that were missed in high school don't really matter anymore.

The irony of being a parent is that the good reasons we have for pushing our children to succeed can, at the same time, lead to behaviors that teach our children to be selfish instead. A parent's greatest strength, his or her steadfast emotional support of the child and the willingness to make sacrifices for that child's athletic advancement, is thus also his or her greatest weakness.

I know you spend a lot of time and money on kids in sports, but don't put too much stress or pressure on your child. Raising kids who are active in sports is hard, perhaps more so today than ever before. As parents we all feel the pressure to help our kids succeed. It's difficult not to want to keep up with other parents. After all, we do live in a winner-take-all society, but it's important to do your best to not become that pushy sports parent. In the end, it may make them resent you and the sport.

I speak from experience. As a father of two children that played basketball, I too have been accused of being a pushy sports parent. One game when my daughter was playing AAU, I can't remember what I said, but I saw it as cheering. Apparently, she saw it as yelling and thought it was a bit much. She called time-out and told her coach that if I was not removed from the gym she would not continue to play. With all eyes on me, my wife politely agreed that maybe I should step out for a while, and so I did, until the game was over. That's just one example, and I'm sure my son could tell you numerous stories about how he had to ride home after the games with me still going over what he could have done better, to the point that he threatened to quit on more than one occasion.

I lightened up after being shocked by their reactions to what I thought was helpful. Like you, I just wanted my kids to excel in everything they did, whatever they decided to do.

My advice is to enjoy the moment, because it doesn't last forever. Kids grow up and move out and move on.

Dianne and I are proud of the fine adults Rashida and Lawrence have grown into. It is so rare these days for the four of us to be together in the same space.

That's why it's important that you enjoy the moments that basketball brings with your kids rather than the game itself, because they won't always be kids. It's the time spent with them that counts. It's about developing closeness and a relationship in which they know they can depend on you, even though they've moved on. I talk to my children almost every day. When the phone rings, I'm just glad to hear their voices. We spend time catching up on what's going in their lives, their careers, and whatever else they want to talk about. That's what I enjoy! I've learned that's what matters the most!

You may be a pushy sports parent if:

1. **You focus on winning more than fully participating.**
   Children who are expected to win are often too anxious to do their best during a game. Additionally, they may lose interest in sports and competition of any kind.
2. **You yell instructions to your child during the game.**
   This only embarrasses your child and adds to the pressure he or she feels. If your child needs some simple feedback, provide it calmly and clearly in a positive way.
3. **You tell your child stories of what you could have become and then push those goals on them.**
   Your time has passed. Remember that your child is a unique person with individual interests and goals, and allow him or her to define his or her own goals.

4. **You make excuses for losing a game.**
   These kids may never learn from their mistakes or try something new because they are quick to blame others for their shortcomings.

If this sounds like you, you can help make sure your child is having fun with the right balance of encouragement and support.

Tips for raising a good sport

1. Encourage your child to try to play any sport he or she enjoys, and support your child's decision *not* to play a sport if he or she doesn't want to.
2. Let your child make mistakes. Doing so is part of learning, and if kids are so afraid of messing up that they quit trying, they unknowingly stop improving.
3. Remind your child of all the health benefits of playing sports
4. Encourage your child to compete against himself, and use competition as a way to improve his own abilities.

Kailah with basketball

Future Star in WNBA—Kialah Rae with basketball

Chapter 6

Teachable

Teachable translates into being coachable. Being coachable is a skill that's just as important as your offensive or defensive skills. It is the one question that every college coach asks doing the recruiting process.

There is no question that the game has changed over the past ten years; more and more kids seem to think that they invented the game and are not overly enthused about being coached.

Kids and parents are more interested in showcasing their own talents and care very little about the team, teammates, and wins or losses. Again, with kids starting at such an early age, they get used to be coddled by their parents and coaches. They are constantly being told how good they are and how much better they are than their opponents or teammates. They really begin to believe the hype. Kids aren't used to dealing with the truth.

Parents sometime really make it difficult for coaches to coach. There are many challenges that coaches face today. One example is that I had a dad that was so adamant about his son being the best player on the team. The kid was only a freshman, but he thought his son deserved major minutes of varsity time. Like many modern-day parents, he even coached his kid from the stands. We lost this kid on day one.

So what exactly is being a coachable player? Well, it starts with recognizing that you don't know everything and being willing to learn. The book of Proverbs says, "In all you do get wisdom and understanding."

It requires humility to admit that you don't have all the answers and to understand that someone can actually teach you something. You must be able to handle constructive criticism, without taking it personal and becoming defensive every time coach says something you don't like or disagree with.

Being coachable requires good listening skills and being attentive. I observe games often where players are doing everything but listen doing the course of a time-out, not realizing that sometimes we only have thirty seconds to teach.

Being coachable is being committed, having the ability to hang in there doing the ups and downs, when things aren't necessarily going the way you'd hoped or planned.

Coachable players want to get better and understand that when they are being coached it's for their own good and the good of the team.

A prime example is that the season prior to Phil Jackson being hired as an assistant coach with the Chicago Bulls, Michael Jordan averaged 37.1 points a game. The first assignment given to the then assistant coach by Doug Collins was to have a discussion with Jordan about helping his team get better. He shared the words of his mentor Red Holzman, his coach with the New York Knicks. One thing that had stuck with Jackson was Red's statement, " It isn't about how great a star player is himself, it's about how great he makes the players around him." Michael, being coachable, transformed his game from being a scorer to learning how to beat teams without having to score. It was the beginning of their championship run. Even the greatest player in the game allowed himself to be coached.

A truly coachable player has the ability to separate the truth from fantasy. I've always told my kids and players that I recognize that its challenging to know who's really in your corner, but "people who want to be your friend, tell you what they think you want to hear; your real friends and those who care about you and tell you the truth, and the truth hurts sometimes."

Characteristics of Great Players

Coach Kevin Eastman, assistant coach with the Boston Celtics, described the characteristics of great players: "I have been so fortunate to be in the NBA and observe the great players. I get to see how they operate and what makes them special. There are certainly others, but here's a list of some separators": (Notice that they allow themselves to be coached.)

- They have tremendous focus on the floor and whenever a coach is talking.
- They want to know anything a coach can give them that will improve their game—always willing to learn.
- They want to get their work in every day.
- They go every bit as hard in practices as they do the games.
- They stay on the practice floor or in the drill until they get it right.
- They know that the little things often separate them from the rest of the players in the league; they pay attention to details.
- They can't stand players that don't work.
- They very seldom sit out of practices.
- They don't mind being corrected and coached when they know the coach is right and the coach is telling them the truth.
- They want to hear the truth.
- They are committed to all aspects of their game—their skills, their bodies, their training, their conditioning, the food they eat … *everything.*
- They hold themselves personally accountable.

- They will also hold their teammates accountable for their roles.
- They despise losing.
- They understand that great players need great teammates; they appreciate team basketball.

Being coachable is a talent that all coaches love because, in the end, as my longtime assistant Christopher "Coach Pete" Johnson says, "You just need to be a sponge."

In the words of John G. Agno, "Once the person commits to being coached, he or she begins to experience a different, more hopeful world as his or her perceptions change.

Lawrence at the University of Minnesota

Courtesy of the University of Minnesota

Chapter 7

Believe

Who would you say is your biggest cheerleader—your mom, your dad, or maybe your grandma?

If you are not your biggest cheerleader, then, "Houston, we have a problem," and you're not ready for liftoff. Your biggest cheerleader has to be you! If you don't believe in you, then why should I or anyone else, for that matter?

During the course of a game, I might hear a young man saying how badly he's playing, how he can't throw the ball into the ocean. When I take him out of the game, and he looks at me like, "What are doing," I tell him, "If you don't believe in what you doing out there, how or why should I?"

I know it's easy to say but hard to do, because believing is about faith, and faith is holding onto that which you can't see. So we are in a constant battle with what we see and with fear of what the situation looks like now.

It's that fear that keeps us from reaching our full potential as we get used to hearing about what we can't do, and why we can't do it. It starts at birth, with you being told don't do this, don't do that, if you do this that will happen. The word *no* is engrained in us. So we learn to play it safe and not to take risks.

The world can be cruel; it places labels on you and tells you that you are not the right color or maybe you don't dress right or maybe you're too short or too big or maybe you talk differently, and we listen to it and start to believe it.

But when you believe in yourself, you have the power to make positive changes. As they say in *Star Trek*, "You can go where man has never gone before."

I'm reminded of this story that I once read called "The Eagle and the Chicken":

A man found an eagle's egg and put it in a nest of a barnyard hen. The eaglet hatched with the brood of chicks and grew up with them. All his life the eagle did what the barnyard chicks did, thinking he was a barnyard chicken.

Years passed and the eagle grew old. One day he saw a magnificent bird above him in the cloudless sky. The old eagle looked up in awe. "Who's that?" he asked.

"'That's the eagle, the king of the birds," said his neighbor.

"He belongs to the sky. We belong to the earth; we're chickens."

So the eagle lived and died as a chicken, for that's what he thought he was.

In short, this is a story about human existence. We are our thoughts. Your mind is your power! We often don't take advantage of the power within us. Why don't we fully use the power of our mind? Because we don't believe in it! We need to learn to believe in the power of the mind or it will not be able to help us. If you want to be successful, then watch your thoughts. Your thoughts determine your attitude, which determine your motivation, which, in turn, determines your accomplishments. Whether you succeed or not is based on your thoughts and beliefs. The ability to think big and be positive is key to your success. Stop thinking like a chicken when you were created to be an eagle!

Think Like a Champion

In October of 1998, I was hired as an assistant coach at Minneapolis Patrick Henry. I was warned that it was a bad job; perhaps if I wanted to coach high school basketball I should go somewhere else. People told me there was no way we could win with kids that lacked discipline and had very little talent. Rumor had it that all of the real ballplayers went to Minneapolis North, Patrick Henry's rival, no, our archenemy would be a more accurate description.

It was true that the school wasn't considered a sports powerhouse, but it had produced some pretty good athletes over the years: Martinez Williams, Leaping Leonard Jones, Prentiss Perkins, and Kelvin Hill, amongst others.

I also took into consideration that we would have some talent returning. We had a five feet ten guard, Mike Pettis, and a six feet eight sophomore, Johnnie Gilbert, who had lots of potential and would later go on to play at the University of Oklahoma.

Coming off a season of being beat in the first round of the sectional play-offs, the school hired a well-known youth pastor who previously coached girl's basketball named Efrem Smith. I was introduced to Efrem in church and asked if he needed any assistants and was offered the opportunity to volunteer.

With him, Efrem brought in a new era at Henry. He coached with Christian principles and shared Bible lessons to back them up. No lesson was greater or more popular than, "I can do all things through Christ who strengthens me. If God be with me, who can be against me?"

In the middle of that first season we were preparing for the first game against our biggest rival, Minneapolis North. Prior to this game they were coming off one of the biggest runs in Minnesota basketball history with three straight state titles, led by standout guard Khalid El-Amin.

Practice that week was challenging, and you could see that our kids' confidence levels were low. It had been a long time since they had beaten Minneapolis North. That week we just kept telling our kids they needed to believe.

It was a Friday night in a crowded gym that our kids began to understand what it meant to believe. Mike Pettis, who was having the game of his life, kept us close, and at the end of regulation every kid in the huddle was shouting, "I believe, I believe." We beat North that night and went on to finish second in the state that year.

Shortly after, Coach Smith left to take a youth pastor job in Dayton, Ohio. I was hired as head coach, and yet a new era began. I knew that beyond talent, our kids needed to believe they could be champions. At our first team retreat, we ended with visualizing being in the state tournament and winning it. We had gotten close, but Minneapolis Patrick Henry still had not won a state title since 1955. I knew, "If we could dream it and believe it, we could achieve it," and they believed. Led by three juniors, Johnnie Gilbert, Greg Patton, and Tony Travis, we would return to the state tournament my first season, only to lose in the quarterfinals that year. The following season would be the beginning of a historical run.

Our mantra "Refuse to Lose" was born, and in 2003, Minneapolis Patrick Henry joined Southwest Minnesota Christian as the only two teams in state history to win four consecutive titles, all because they learned to *believe*!

MSHSL 2000 State Champions
Class AAA Boys Basketball

2000

Championship Team

Chapter 8

Attitude

Your attitude can either be your greatest asset or your greatest liability. We often speak about an athlete having the heart of a champion, but what really matters is having the head of a champion.

It is the foundation of becoming a champion, whether on the court, in the classroom, in the community, or in your family.

One attitude is critical to the type of player you become, but more important is the type of person you become.

What exactly is attitude? Webster defined attitude as, "A manner of thinking, acting, and feeling." So if attitude is your thoughts, what you do always starts with what and how you think.

Everybody wants to be a champion, but so few people really know how. It's been written that 85 percent of a person's success is attributed to one's attitude, and 15 percent to the skills that he or she has developed.

For so many coaches the emphasis is skill development, and very little time is spent on developing the right attitude and character.

I often reminded my teams that we won 90 percent of our games before we ever took the court, simply because teams didn't believe that they could beat us, and we didn't believe that we could be beaten.

A common ritual in our locker room was to repeat after me, "I'm a winner. I'm a warrior. I'm a champion. I refuse to lose. I am the best—I am the best offensive player; I am the best defensive player. I am the best; I refuse to lose."

Our daily practice of a positive mental attitude was our reciting what became known as the Patriot creed; we repeated it before every practice and every game. I always told our players that if they didn't take anything else out of what we were doing on the court and didn't remember a thing I ever said, always remember our creed.

"This is the beginning of a new day; God has given me this day to use as I will—I waste it or use it for good. For what I do today is important; I am exchanging a day of my life for it. I want it to be good not bad, gain not loss, success not failure, in order that I will never regret the price that I paid for it."

This creed was first shared with me by my younger brother, John, while he was a head football coach at Delaware State University. I repeated it daily with relatively little understanding, until one day I learned that one of my best friends had died from breast cancer. Myra was forty years old, and, like so many, I thought she would be here forever.

It immediately hit how every morning was God's gift to me and to each of the young men that God had placed in my care, so I begin to really break it down so that it would have greater meaning to them.

This is the beginning of a new day: As I already mentioned, every day is a gift from God; it is a day that has never been and a day that never will be again, so don't take it for granted. I was reminded through reading the obituary column that there are those that were with us yesterday, that are not here today.

God have given me this day to use as I will: Each day God makes a deposit of 86,400 seconds into our life account, and no matter how much I love my wife, son, and daughter, or they love their mother, father, sister or brother, they couldn't share it.

Know that each of us was responsible for what happened during that day and not somebody else.

I can waste it or use it for good: We all know people who waste time, whose mantra is, "I'll get done tomorrow." Frankly, I have been there myself. Just as we had team goals, they needed personal goals. We discussed that when you don't have goals, you lack accountability, and how unfortunate it is that most people just live life; they go through their days and lives with no destination in mind, so wherever the journey takes them is okay. Being average is what God gives us when we awaken every morning, and at the end of those 86,400 seconds, something good should have happened.

For what I do today is important: Because it is a gift, and we are a gift, every day we don't reach our maximum potential there are consequences, such as not taking care of business in the classroom would impact their eligibility, and they wouldn't be able to help the team, and they would lose scholarships and not have the opportunity to play at the next level.

)The decisions we make at fourteen or fifteen not only impact us, but also impact our kids, our grandkids, and some girl that they probably didn't know already.

I am exchanging a day of my life for it: We take it for granted that we have forever, but tomorrow truly is not promised. They all had the option of doing other things, but if your goal is to be a champion in anything, it requires sacrifice. Somebody once told me, "Champions are willing to do what nobody else is willing to do." They come early and leave late, sacrifice a new suit so you can have the latest sneakers, man up and take care of their offspring, and say no to their friends to study and pass that exam.

I want it to be good not bad: It starts with waking up, and there is no such thing as getting up on the wrong side of the bed. It's not in the breakfast of champions, but I'm responsibility for me. It's not about blaming teachers for grades or coaches for playing time. I understand that nobody can push my hot button, as we call it, unless I allow it. If I want it, I have to go get it, and it may not be easy.

Gain not loss: Every day should be a step toward that goal of being a champion on the court, in the classroom, and in your family and community. I want more playing time, but I can't shoot free throws. How can I work on my free throws today? What can I do to go from 60 percent to 70 percent? My goal is to go to a certain school. What grade point do I need? Can I do extra credit to go from a C to a B? Don't wait for mom to tell you to take out the garbage; give your sister a hug. Sit at the lunch table with that one student who always eats by himself or herself. Be a difference maker.

Success not failure: One of our requirements in order to try for the team was for our guys to run a six-minute mile. It was as much about goal setting as it was about conditioning. With the satisfaction of knowing that each kid in the huddle was in peak condition, I would often ask the question or have them run it again to see if they could do better. My question would be, "Did you really do your best?" If you really pushed on that last quarter mile, could you get to 5:58 or maybe 5:55? Every player would respond by saying yes and would agree that you could always do better than your best. Our success also increased in the classroom, going from a team grade point of 1.6 to 3.4 over five years.

Our goal was always to be the last team playing, and four out of five years we achieved that goal. For us, failure was not an option.

In order that I would never regret the price we paid for it: I always reminded my kids that they could be working to help support their families, as many of them were from single-parent homes, or be home playing Playstation, chasing girls, or running the streets, but instead they made a commitment to come to school every morning at 6:00 a.m. to lift weights and run, and stayed after school from September through June for mandatory study hall.

Their summers consisted of regular workouts and playing more games while their peers worked earning spending money or went on family vacations.

If you are going to do all of this and make such a commitment, "Use the game; don't let the game use you. It is a tremendous price to pay with no return."

Keith Harrell, in his book *Attitude Is Everything*, writes that attitude is more important than facts. The one thing that we have a choice about every day is our attitude—how we embrace every morning.

Life is 10 percent of what happens and 90 percent of how we react to it.

2003 championship team

MINNESOTA HIGH SCHOOL 2003 CLASS AAA BOYS BASKETBALL

FINAL RECORD	STATE QUARTERFINALS		STATE SEMIFINALS		STATE FINALS	
26-6	Patrick Henry	76	Patrick Henry	59	Patrick Henry	69
	Totino-Grace	55	Red Wing	54	Sauk Rapids-Rice	55

UN-FOUR-GETABLE!

Patriots join elite company by becoming just second school to win 4 straight state titles

Minneapolis Patrick Henry joined Southwest Minnesota Christian as the only two schools to win four consecutive Minnesota boys basketball titles when the Patriots downed Sauk Rapids-Rice 69-55 to capture the 2003 Class AAA championship.

Patrick Henry led by just two points at the half, 36-34, but blew the game open in the third quarter by outscoring Sauk Rapids-Rice 26-13.

Lawrence McKenzie and Calvin Walls each scored 20 points to lead the way for the Patriots. Walls also grabbed 11 rebounds and McKenzie pulled down seven boards. Steve Neal had 15 points and six rebounds.

In the semifinals, a rematch of the 2002 championship game, Patrick Henry led by as many as 17 points in the fourth quarter only to see Red Wing cut that lead to four with 33 seconds to play before the Patriots closed out the game at the free-throw line. Walter Power had a game-high 17 points and McKenzie added 15.

2003 PATRICK HENRY PATRIOTS ROSTER AND RESULTS

Chapter 9

Love to Live

It's a song that resonates in my spirit. I first heard it sung by George Benson; it later became a megahit when sung by Whitney Houston. It's called, "The Greatest Love of All." The chorus says, "The greatest love of all is easy to achieve; learning to love yourself is the greatest love of all."

Loving to live starts with the understanding that each of us is truly special, made in the image of our creator, so special that there is no one else that has our identical fingerprints. We indeed are not one in a million, but are that one special person amongst billions.

When you love to live you understand that it begins with the choices you make—whether you choose to lead or to follow; the choice of your thoughts, whether they are positive or negative; your friends; and the people that you associate with.

I often say that the older I get the more nursery rhymes make sense, and it's true that birds of a feather stick together. Successful people want to be around successful people, while misery loves company.

I read once that if you want to be a millionaire, find one to hang out with, and it makes sense, because they're making deals with people like themselves. My kids and my players have heard me say a thousand times that misery loves company.

Isn't it funny that with the guys or girls that aren't playing, it's always the coach's fault. In the locker room, it's them always complaining that the coach doesn't know what he's doing. And they never complain to the starters but to the other kids on the bench.

The ones who aren't getting done in the classroom always complain about why their grades are being checked. Or maybe they are failing with a big project due, and they invite you to a party for the weekend.

In the Bible, 1 Corinthians, 15:33says that if those who are not corrupt hang out with those that are corrupt, eventually they become corrupt.

Surround yourself with dream makers not dream killers, not those whose only contribution to you is to bring nothing but negative energy.

The choices that we make sometimes are really game changers, not only on the court but also in the game of life. I understand the pain of young people making bad choices; one of my former players is currently serving life without parole in a California prison. The sad thing is that it only takes fifteen- to twenty-second lapses in judgment to ruin your life and change your future.

Terry Pettis was an outstanding student-athlete who excelled in football and basketball—a star quarterback and a three-time state champion in basketball at Minneapolis Patrick Henry. He had star qualities, and he earned a basketball scholarship to attend Fresno State in pursuit of playing in the NBA. Like a lot of my players, he had his daily challenges, but no one ever considered him a murderer.

But in a split second, in what was described as a botched robbery, a young lady was killed, and his life and all of those who were connected to him and to her were forever changed.

Young people today are faced with challenges that I couldn't even imagine—the lure of hip-hop culture, the information superhighway, and the influence of music videos and mass media.

Loving to live is not only valuing your life, but also the lives of others, and somehow when you love yourself it makes it that much more difficult for you to take another life. You understand that guns are used to kill or to be killed. The sad thing in this country is that a firearm kills eight children or teens every day.

Richard Pryor used to say, "You don't get old by being no fool." Giving yourself a chance to get older allows you to become wiser. When you are young you make decisions with little or no regard to how you might be affected years from now.

When you love to live, what you eat and don't eat becomes important. Your diet becomes crucial in your long-term success at this game. After all, it is your resume; it's how you make your first impression on a coach. If you don't take care of your body, it won't take care of you.

A lot of players learn the important of good nutrition too late. I must admit that I've only recently begun to understand that eating correctly can prevent heart disease, strokes, and cancer. Not only is your diet important but so are proper sleep and exercise.

Without sounding preachy, when you love to live, you know that you cannot put chemicals into your body. You don't let peer pressure cause you to try alcohol or drugs.

I know you see other athletes who do it, but I'm not convinced that they will tell you that it's good for you. I'm not an expert, but there is no way you can perform at your maximum potential if you are high on something.

If you truly love the game and yourself, you will do whatever it takes to get where you want to go.

Rev. Pauline Jones 100th Birthday

Chapter 10

Live to Love

In a 1968 speech in Atlanta, the late Dr. Martin Luther King Jr. spoke the words, "Everybody can be great because everybody can serve." He went on to say, "You don't have to have a college degree to serve. You don't need to know about Plato or Aristotle to serve. You only need a heart full of grace, a soul generated by love."

It is the true essence of living to love; it means that everybody can be a difference maker—you don't have to be rich and famous or have special credentials.

For as long as I can remember, I watched my family embrace sharing and giving, even though we didn't always have a lot. My grandmother, Pauline Jones, a very spiritual woman, was there for anybody with need, whether in the church or in the community.

My grandfather, William Jones, served as the neighborhood handyman. Gifted with the ability to turn wood into a masterpiece, he gave both his time and talent.

As for my mom and dad, Lawrence and Retha McKenzie, an open house had a different meaning for us growing up. Our house was where relatives and friends came to relax, to get a meal, or to lay their heads. They silently taught my siblings and me that life was about lifting people up and lending a helping hand. It is probably is the reason that my brother John and I are coaching, making a difference in the lives of the young men that we're blessed to have in our lives. My sister Paula is a nurse, helping those that are sometimes in their weakest moments, and my sister Carla is an administrator with the school system. But, more importantly, while not having any biological kids of her own, she has become an adoptive mother and grandmother.

I have been blessed to marry a woman with the same values and upbringing. So, as fate would have it, we would end up taking my niece and nephew after my wife lost her sister to sickle cell anemia.

My nephew would move to Minneapolis seeking a better education; we would become foster parents, along with opening our doors to a few of my players who would move in.

Very early in life, Rashida and Lawrence would learn to share their parents just we learned to share ours.

When you live to love, you understand having the responsibility of leaving this earth a much better place than you found it.

Sometimes it is as simple as saying good morning or walking past someone with a smile on your face.

Maybe it's sitting down for lunch with the kid that nobody else wants sit with or inviting him or her over for the sleepover.

The true essence of living to love is a feeling of selflessness, turning me into we, and them into us, and giving, not always receiving. There are those that make things happen, those who watch things happen, and those who wonder what happened.

I once heard a sermon preached called "The Dash." It was simple yet profound. I later found that the sermon was taken from the poem of Linda Ellis.

The Dash
by Linda Ellis

There was a man who stood to speak
At the funeral of a friend
He referred to the dates on her tombstone
From the beginning to the end

He noted that first came her date of her birth
And spoke the following date with tears
But he said what mattered most of all
Was the dash between those years

For that dash stands for all the time
That she spent alive on earth.
And now only those who loved her
Know what that little line is worth.

For it matters not how much we own;
the cars, the house, the cash
What matters is how we live and love
And how we spend our dash.

So think about this long and hard.
Are there things you'd like to change?
For you never know how much time is left
That can still be rearranged.

If we could just slow down enough
To consider what's true and real
And always try to understand
The way other people feel.

We'd be less quick to anger
And show appreciation more
And love the people in our lives
Like we've never loved before.

If we treat each other with respect
And more often wear a smile
Remembering that this special dash
Might only last a little while.

So when your eulogy is being read
With your life's actions to rehash
Would you be proud of the things they say
About how you spent your dash?

Cos that dash stands for all the time
That you spent alive on earth
And only those who loved you
Know what that little line is worth

It matters not how much you own
The cars, the house, the cash
What matters is how you live and love
And how you spend your dash

What matters is how you live and love
And how you spend your dash.

So when that final horn sounds, and you've scored that last basket in
the game of life, I hope your final stats will read as you being the type
of player who not only had the ability to score, but was always willing to
provide an assist, and your dash will say you were truly a champion.

Rashida wedding with four generations of the Jones-McKenzie Family

Larry A. McKenzie
Biography

Larry A. McKenzie is currently going into his fourth season as the head coach of Academy of Holy Angels. He was formerly general manager and head coach of the Minnesota Ripknees of the American Basketball Association (ABA). In their first season, the Ripknees clinched the title of division champions, with a winning record of 24–8.

Prior to joining the Minnesota Ripknees, Larry A. McKenzie served as head coach for the Minneapolis Patrick Henry boys' basketball team for nine seasons.

In nine seasons, Coach McKenzie and his staff developed the Patriots into one of the nation's top high school programs.

Under his leadership the Patriots won four consecutive Class AAA state titles, five Region 5 AAA titles, three Twin Cities titles, and six consecutive Minneapolis City Conference titles, finishing with an overall record of 202–34.

Prior to the arrival of Coach McKenzie and his staff, the Patriots had not won a state title in fifty-five years. Under McKenzie's direction, the Patriots established themselves as a team dedicated to hard work, tenacious defense, and a high-octane offense.

McKenzie's mission was to develop a championship program while also using basketball as a tool to empower young men to be champions in their classrooms, families, and communities.

By developing a highly structured program and a group of dedicated young coaches, the team showed tremendous improvement in the classroom, increasing the team GPA from 1.6 to a 3.1. In just two years, 95 percent of the players had made the A or B honor roll.

Under Coach McKenzie's leadership, all of the Patriots' seniors were enrolled in an institution of higher learning, with the majority playing college basketball.

Just a few of Coach McKenzie's many accolades include being named section and region coach of the year three consecutive years: 1999, 2000, and 2001. In 2001 he was also named Class AAA Coach of the Year and was selected by the NFHSC as Minnesota Basketball Coach of the Year.

A native of Miami, McKenzie currently resides in Minneapolis, Minnesota, with his wife, Dianne. He is the father of two children, Rashida McKenzie-Ogunride and Lawrence McKenzie, and is the grandpa to Kailah Rae McKenzie.

AHA Coaching

Coach McKenzie

"Inspiring Youth To Champions"

Need a speaker for your upcoming event?

A coach, educator, author, and speaker, Larry McKenzie, the only coach to win four straight state titles in the ninety-nine year history of the Minnesota State Boys Basketball Tournament, is sharing his success strategies for "winning" on the court and in life. Coach McKenzie shows why BASKETBALL is merely a metaphor and a tool that can be used to transform lives.

Coach Larry McKenzie has the winning words and strategies for your business, church, school, or organization. Larry successfully inspires and motivates audiences everywhere to enjoy, achieve, and go from the sidelines to become true players for your business, church, school, or organization.

www.CoachMcKenzie.com

(763) 458-5450

Bibliography

Aron, Jamie. "Current, former NBA players aiming to improve AAU." *Yahoo Sports*, 11 June 2010. http://sports.yahoo.com/nba/news.

Brown, Randy. "Skill Development Checklist." http://Coachrb.com.

Crawford, Bryan. "Corruption in Amateur Athletics." *Slamonline*, 24 August 2009. http:www.slamonline/online/college-hs/college 2009/08.

Eastman, Kevin. "Characteristic of a great player." http://kevineastmanbasketball.com.

Ellis, Linda. "The Dash." Simple Truth 2005

Forde, Pat. "Adults, shoe companies joust over elite teens,"12 October 2005, ESPN.com. http://sports.espn.go.com/espn/print.

Harrell, Keith "Attitude Is Everything" FirstHarperBusiness 2003

Helyar, John. "Basketball Getting Dunked in Las Vegas Cesspool." http://www.bloomberg.com/apps/news.

Hohler, Bob. "Are You Kidding?" *The Boston Globe*, 25 July 2006. http://www.boston.com/sports/basketball/articles/.

Issenberg, Marc. "College hoops must look within before assigning blame elsewhere." *Basketball Times*: 17. July 2010

Liberalamerican. "The Strange Death of Liberal America: March Madne$$," 15 March 2009.

Naismith, James Dr. "History of Basketball." Kansas Heritage Group. http://www.kansashertiage.org/people/naismith.html.

Pessah, Jon. "The Godfather of Basketball Is Writing a New Ending," 30 July 2007. http://sports.espn.go.com.

Wentzel, Dan. "Agents and AAU: Unrequited Love," 11 March 2009, Yahoo Sports.com. http://rivals.yahoo.com/ncaa/basketball/news,.

Weiner, Jay and Steve Berkowitz. "What players get: $120K a year." *USA Today,* 30 March 2011.

Wynn, Mychal. *Building Dreams: Helping Students Discover Their Potential*. Rising Sun Publishing, 1994.

Made in the USA
Lexington, KY
02 March 2012